T0381152

CLAUDIA A KRIZAY

A Tree
GROWS
IN SECLUSION

To order additional copies of this book, contact:
Xlibris
844-714-8691
www.Xlibris.com
Orders@Xlibris.com

ISBN: 978-1-6698-7313-6 (sc)
ISBN: 978-1-6698-7314-3 (e)

Print information available on the last page

Rev. date: 04/04/2023

To all people living with disabilities.

Contents

A Tree Grows In Seclusion 2

Upon this morning I must abandon this world-
My cry for help cannot not be silenced-

Wrathful skies have just hurled meteors-
I can hear thunder roar-
Archangels in the sky have displayed their fury.

After a storm has abated- calmed by a gentle breeze,
I sense that I have stumbled upon rhapsody's doorstep.

The revitalization of glowing clouds adorned in lavender skylight
Is a most mesmerizing vision to behold.

Locked inside of this dungeon
where there paradoxically exists an escape from the horrors of my imagination,
leaves from a flourishing tree quiver in a tenacious breeze-

Raindrops consume the sunlight-
Once reflecting massive and catastrophic panic.

Encased within some lone and dazzling asteroid existing in some remote galaxy-
I foresee a spirited tree emerging from this worn and tainted carpet-
A shadow of my past, although an inspiration for a future.

Dewdrops are translucent pearls dancing atop leaves
upon this exquisite tree, becoming tiny stages-
above this place where petals of silver toned wild roses are applauding.

Flight of my imagination carries me beyond these weathered walls.
Visions that appear when my thoughts spiral about and beyond my control-
And the discordant tunes that play rampantly inside of my mind-
Become as entrancing as agile figures dancing to some distant but melodious orchestra…

A tranquil image emerges from the dreamscape I have painted
Upon the once sallow tinted walls of my imagination
Where stellar studded rainbows shall evolve over time….

Claudia A Krizay

After a Storm

Pearlescent shards of terror are scattered about roads towards nowhere
reflecting ferocious sky lightning still eminent from eyes of strangers.

Peering from behind graphite hued clouds
terrified grimaces of disarray stare into newly formed oceans
deep as a dungeon at the core of this planet…

Humanoid creatures envision their contorted reflections
stretched as grimaces in fun house mirrors-consumed by snakes and alligators –
no room exists for compassion from this aftermath…

Bleeding guts of victims flow into rivers of catastrophe
Waters turning crimson and decomposing bodies
Float like helium balloons upon seas of terror
Voices emanating from the center of gravity
Are calling out to desperate spirits In the bleakness of this night

Demons are laughing cacophonously-
Possessed by evil sorcerers who have stolen away this night.
Nobody cares about love and salvation
In a world that is imploding and sinking into bedlam-
Lost and forgotten souls are weeping-
They cry, they worship a God that does not care-

Wind carries shadows towards hell where wild birds and high grasses have perished-
Fallen trees and burning foundations of wrath-
God's broken promises and voices of angels, forsaken.
Tears of terrified children are splashing upon
Translucent and murky ponds of disarray - alone in their plight.

An eerie vibrato settles over miles of calamity and despair-
Moss covered walkways and slimy foundations-
People are hiding from shades of oblivion with no recourse from fear.

This moment is still as stagnant waters where victims have woefully drowned.
A lone creature cries out-remaining as none, but a silhouette ravaged by the wind-

Thunder claps. angels of the deceased are weeping from darkening skies above
as they peer from behind graphite hued clouds- silent as phantoms in the eye of this storm-
still as this night on these roads that lead towards nowhere….

Claudia A Krizay

After the Skies have Imploded

When skies implode I am left alone screaming with raucous joy,
loudly as a glass tower falling and hitting cragged rocks-
I leap, though cautiously into open space.

When skies are imploding, doors have been unchained
Allowing me to escape billions of others in which I place no trust-

I am drowning in a deluge, lost inside of a hostile world,
sinking into the sea without hope upon which to grasp-

Somehow I am finding myself very much alive
Cavorting amongst meteor showers and falling stars,
After everyone has perished.

The skies have imploded, and I have come upon a rock of silvered granite
Upon which to grasp and embrace, after the world has mysteriously vanished-

Stars are tiny fairies with iridescent wings,
Waltzing amongst stark white cumulous clouds near dusk-
I behold their exquisiteness as they dance within my open arms-
The centers of trillions of galaxies –

I have never believed in angels,
Although I do believe in fate and often, magic-
I believe in the guidance of the stars.

There exists a special revitalizing star, to become the center of a galaxy of my creation-
Where I shall stand alone to chant my own tuneful and arousing melodies.

I have become the center of a spellbinding aura
that revitalizes my spirit in the darkness past the midnight hours-

I whisper with raucous joy, loudly as a straight pin falling from a hidden mountaintop
And quietly shattering upon the silvered granite rock of my salvation-
where I devour peace of mind, only after the skies have risen, then imploded…

Claudia A Krizay

Amazing As this Night

Amazing as this night-
The moon and stars play games with sparsely scattered light.

Stellar mysticism is gently rising-
Eerily gleaming and almost hypnotizing.

At the dawning I have been set free but still fearing the night-
Demons are rising from within me and valiantly armed to fight-

At the sunrise I perceive a shrouded sorcerer slyly coming alive
Stealing the light away without which I feel cannot survive-

My spirit once alive is now filled with indefinable wrath and doubt
Leaving me to wonder what living is truly about.

The essence of my existence rises as a flamboyant eagle taking flight-
Amazing as this night.

I peer through dense fog and can faintly see stars in motion colliding-
While fear and anguish are inexplicably subsiding.

As I witness shades of a rainbow emanate as an aura about the soundlessly emerging moon,
I perceive living beings from other galaxies chanting harmonious choruses in tune-

Stellar illumination forms an awesome and extraordinary glow-
Illuminating my dreams and unveiling the magic of what we do not truly know.

I sense a revelation within my soul never far removed, but now distinctively near-
A miraculous dream has left me alone with more to learn and much less to fear.

Demons of the darkness have become angels robed in iridescent light-
Darkened skies interspersed with gilded stardust become a most astonishing sight-
Amazing as this night…

Claudia A Krizay

Autumn Dawning

At every dawning amidst the heart of autumn
clouds that are illuminated by a stray beam of sunlight- are bursting through
Deepening rain clouds, slate-gray and elusive.

Wrath seethes inside of my mind-
I weep amidst thunder though in a whispering stillness.

As the night passes,
A shimmering curtain opens gently and without fear
To allow peeks of daylight to cautiously slip through
An open crack in my bedroom window-

My spirit evades me, at the break of day- A cool and gentle breeze
Tiptoes through that open crack in my bedroom window-
As the sky, transforms to a magnificent shade of cyanotic blue-

If dragonflies could sing arias
As they hover about trees outside of my window
I would join them in harmony within this rare moment in time-
To be healed by their musical intonations-

Alone with my thoughts, I allow the light of my imagination
To expand throughout the perimeters this room

An obscure type of sorcery is somehow woven within a fine net of my creation
that captures the remnants of the anger that now lingers
and had plagued past nights.

Tranquility, would become a cleansing rain
that leaks through that open crack in my bedroom window
with utmost pleasure and conviction.

This extraordinary moment has given me a gift
Of the delicate aroma of phantasmal carnations and blossoming peonies
to overshadow the fear that has for a lifetime tormented me.

Alone with my thoughts, the spirit that has been robbed of its peace of mind-
heals and rejuvenates as tears wept for rage furtively slip away
as darkness disperses into the heart of an autumn dawning…

Claudia A Krizay

Betrayed by Light

My world darkens as light surrounds me-
A wall has been erected between myself and this world-
Light surrounds me- I cannot reach.
I search the same path that I walk everyday-

Light surrounds me, my dreams embellish:
A sky without cloudiness,
Trees that grow tall and strong bearing blossoms that shall never fall?
Light surrounds me- darkness interrupts.
I am sinking inside of puddles of massive confusion,

Light surrounds me, the light I had often believed to be the light of promises,
The light of good fortune, the light of survival.
Light has smoldered within my tree of hope-
The light of treachery and broken promises.

I mourn for every tree that has fallen, perished
And has been ravished by a tempest of rage.
Reflecting light encompasses me and sears the core of my existence-
That fallen tree casts blinding shadows, obliterating my horizon.

I seek refuge through the mystifying haziness,
I am chanting melodies of rejuvenated dreams-
As sunlight bursts through bleak fog in all of its crystalline clarity-

I frolic within a fleeting instant atop mountains of madness-
before toxic rain falls quenching flames of illumination.
Darkness interrupts, profoundly and brusquely.

The blossoms once alive upon that fallen tree have perished
And have been carried away by the wicked force of wind.
Rekindling within a different frame of time and place…
My world has darkened. Stars have burnt out light years away.

Light surrounds me- the light of darkness-
I foresee a spark ignite within a distant sky-
A spark that is rapidly reducing to ashes.

I stand erect amidst blackening mayhem
Darkness surrounds me- betrayed by the light.

Claudia A Krizay

Beyond Velvet Cirrus Clouds

Heaven awaits those who die young,
my mother's apparitional words-
Those who die young find their homes in paradise.

My father died young.
His spirit had been fabricated
From impenetrable obsidian stone- so dark, so cold-

Lurking behind a sky of blackened steel,
Dank and callous,
My father had often struck me
With his knuckles of wrought iron- my blood runs cold.

Before the setting of the sun,
The skies become a rare shade of cobalt blue-
At the sunrise, magenta and violet hued.
It has been said that heaven awaits beyond velvet cirrus clouds.

My father died young-
Perhaps his wicked spirit found its way beyond those clouds…

My mother died young- I never found her heart,
Lost within her tortured soul.
I still hear her weeping past the midnight's hours.

Perhaps my mother has found solace within
That magical heaven of hope
she used to tell me bedtime tales about.

My mother and father died young.
Perhaps someday I shall meet with them once again
In that paradise beyond velvet cirrus clouds
After my own life has ended,
Although I have never believed in magic.

When thunder claps, I hear my father
Striking hearts of angels amongst the skies, with his knuckles of wrought iron.

It has been said that people never change, not even after they leave this world.
I believe I shall live forever…

Claudia A Krizay

Breakdown

Seated cross-legged upon a wooden beamed floor-
I pray to the Goddess, the savior of my spirit
Fabricated in a moment, lost, and forgotten-
Now I speak only to the people who have passed.

Beyond the mountains, violet in their hue-
And the loveliness of crimson clouds-
Speak to me only of yesterday.
While a ghost-like shadow eradicates the light,
the presence of faltering footsteps louden, and indistinct tones resonate.

I have thrown my innermost thoughts into a blazing fire past the midnight hour.
In this moment of terrifying madness I pray to the goddess, the savior of my spirit-
The burnt out candle that still guides me-
Towards a place where I look about but cannot see.

Crimson clouds transform to dank and slate colored fogginess
As ashes fall from a bleak and threatening sky-
This rare sort of rain cascades downward…

Lightening is a heartbeat monitor reverberating
while thunder resounds against iron- clad walls
that fabricate this lurid planet.

There is no magic beyond violet mountains
And crimson clouds are elements of reveries past.
Matchsticks pound upon a base drum
Igniting all harmonious sounds transforming into bedlam.

I weep bitter tears that sear my eyes-
My eyes that see but cannot fathom
Or discern what is true from the visions I foresee..

Shackles are boa constrictors
That bind my wrists as my thoughts become misconstrued.
The aura of the goddess of my past
Has faded into the mysticism of an unknown galaxy-

I find myself alone in the bleak darkness of this chamber of disarray-
I forlornly reach out to collect sporadically falling ashes
from crimson clouds that have dissipated into the cosmos of the midnight hours.
Cherished moments in time have been stolen away by a conniving wizard of the night….

Claudia A Krizay

15

Breaking Away

Within a dream, perhaps a shadow would pass me by,
Or a fawn would wade in the creek alongside of the path I walk-
I would break away from reality if only there was a point of no return…

I can look down upon this pathway
Where evergreens and birch trees are questioning the skies.
Fireflies are hovering above the treetops-I would dance with them
in my fondest aspirations…

Beyond firmaments of cobalt blue past the twilight hours,
The sun behind me is casting shadows
that are steadily transforming to distant fantasies
of an eternal life inside this world of my own-

Here, I can listen to the litheness of nature surrounding me,
the sound of my heart beating amorously,
And to my own shadow stepping in time to
myriads of towering oak trees attempting to graze the skies-
I had locked that gate that confines all that is real.

Dozens of humanoid creatures had been pacing behind
My silhouette that had become endangered
crossing that pathway I fearfully wandered.

In flight of my imagination
There would be no turning back- even if it was only within a hypnogogic moment-
Where I would find myself trapped amidst cacophony and disaster,
that can be found in my own back yard.

A gust of wind could momentarily strike that gateway
and allow an upsurge of ghostly intruders
that could threaten all I have ever imagined, where misfortune is painfully on the rise-

I serenely follow the shadows cast by the sun- so intriguingly amazing,
That would overshadow any nightmarish vision.

I would never look backwards
But only further towards the skies, where treetops proudly reign.
Starlings would chant heart wrenching but exquisite melodies-

I am finding myself breakdancing alone with fireflies, illuminating the night….

Claudia A Krizay

Broken Promise

My world darkens as
sunlight encompasses me--
blinding me
with its daunting and deceitful fury.

Upon a pathway, seemingly endless,
sunlight envelops my shadow like a sequined shawl-
dazzling and fearless-

A cobalt blue sky has been anchored to the shoreline
Where the garish light of the sun
Sears mountains of madness,
encircled by pools of massive confusion.

My world ceases to orbit
about the sun that had once promised to guide me.

Hope dwindles.
Lightering strikes
Arousing my shadow,
Now sinking into oblivion
then seeping through mystifying haziness

Mountains of madness become volcanoes erupting
igniting my spirit,
once lost some place inside of my shrouded world.

The light of the sun
Has been none but a lie.
Replete with vengeance and broken promises-
Dissolving into toxic rain-
Now raging alone in the darkness.

Stars, cascading-
Peeks of illumination-
Are breaking through immaculate skies
of a deepening cyanotic blue…

Claudia A Krizay

Circle

I am very much alive within the center of a circle,
Here, grasses grow high, and magical weeping willow trees
come to life to give me shelter.

My circle confines me, and protects me
From the outside world-
Inside of my circle I have found a home and a refuge from intruders.

Outside of my circle, glorious skies of azure blue have lied to me
and astonishing rainbows have been untrue
As they tell me that life outside of my circle is bright and promising
when in actuality, is dark and threatening.

Inside of my circle, I live my life in solitude,
Where I sing with the choruses of archangels of my creation.

My home for nearly twenty years has become the circle of my well-being,
Where the walls are decorated with painted canvases of my imagination-

My knitted woolen blanket, though torn and yellowed with age
Warmly wraps about me and protects me
from the bitter cold of midwinter storms that ravage the world outside-

Soothing voices that only I can hear
Tenderly whisper their harmonious words to me-
Encased within my circle I can joyously dance alone.

Inside of this place where sea green grasses grow high,
Both daylight and starlight can radiate from within-

What makes this place inside of my circle a most special kingdom
Is that it is of my own creation,
Of which I shall always be the center.

Claudia A Krizay

Collision

The day that an asteroid collided with the planet earth,
and many of the stars had vanished- was a day when all music halted-

Frantically grasping at every note, subsiding
where starlings once chanted their mournful arias-
I once had written my life's story in a song.

Darkening clouds sharply contrasted
with the skies of a deepening cobalt blue.
There was a moment that my thoughts had been misconstrued..

Stillness rang throughout the universe
Where I fabricated angels that only I could love and trust.

We spoke our own aberrant language
Inaudible to people who had roamed the earth,
But somehow the tallest trees could always hear us.

The moment that my shadow stopped screaming,
I fell into a state of complete oblivion, but captured my spirit dancing,
Within a net of iridescent magic, woven within fine silken threads.

Upon that day a voice inside of me
Whispered to me that miracles could happen-
I was reborn into a very unique, but distant world.

I could see that rainbows were swaying
On that very mysterious day in time.

My hands would reach for the skies
As I painted my world with even and determined brushstrokes
Upon a canvas of my fantasies.

When I would laugh I could not be heard,
As I was locked inside of a bizarre but wondrous chamber of madness.
It was on that very day that my voice had been silenced.

That day that I abandoned veracity,
Was the day that asteroid collided
With the planet I had left behind…

Claudia A Krizay

Confidence

To be alone amongst nature at nightfall carries a sense of omnipotence within.
In the midwinter my silhouette has been cast, then mirrored in an ice-clad pond.

I worship my reflection when silence chants an aria
In tune with snowflakes dancing as tiny particles of shattered glass.
Shards turn iridescent before my eyes amidst starkly barren trees.

Alone on a summer's evening gazing upward towards the skies
my spirit consumes the starlight.

Cherishing a unique and special horizon carries my thoughts towards another realm.
I gracefully chase my shadow to find my dreams coming to life-

Spring rain begins to fall upon the pathway towards my paradise-
I rejoice in my solitude as crystalline droplets cleanse my soul of fear-

I listen to the quiet of the early morning summoning me to climb that gilded stairway
That leads to a safe haven that has been erected for me, alone.

Dreams are bountiful. Visions of aloneness
Are exquisite as I become the artist In control of my existence.
The spirit of living becomes a gift from the heavens.

To love oneself is an astonishing God given gift,
Where I become the sun that sets with utmost confidence
Then rising once again to enlighten that world of my creation.

I stand with self-assurance painting the skies a softened shade of cerulean blue,
And pearl white cirrus clouds scattered above magenta-peaked mountain tops.
Chartreuse tinted grasses are growing high, and wild violets
are flourishing as far as I can envision-

Serenity forms a symphony composed for me, alone.
I silently whisper in tune to the magic of a gentle breeze
Upon this extraordinary starlit night.

Claudia A Krizay

Dying

(To my mother on the 30th anniversary of her death, December 4th)

You lie still as a sadly fallen birch tree
Weeping alone in a vast and deep forest
from which you do not care to awaken.

As I gently fondle a strand of your refined silver hair
I would wonder in this fleeting and desperate moment-
Did you not trust the wind when the skies were trembling?
Or when the clouds shuddered and dissipated
Like a flame on a candlewick that burned to the ground?

As I gently touch your wrist and call your name,
I can see a frozen smile appearing -and your eyes, closed to the world outside-
That world that threatens your existence.

When you took your final breath
I recalled how you never trusted the wind, the rain or the changing of time-
You only trusted the voices of the past-
I remember I had seen you lithe as a newborn starling
Chanting high pitched songs welcoming a world
That you knew nothing about?

Still as this night- you become lifeless as a tree fallen after a squall,
Now hollow as your lonesome spirit has escaped-
Perhaps your soul is lost inside the amity of a fawn,
Shy and nimble but thankful for all the forest has to give…

Darkness is descending as the stars seek refuge behind the fog-
Perhaps your spirit shall return as a flamingo dancing
Near the waters, jubilant to see its reflection.

I can feel your pain and anguish stab me as would a tainted spear,
As your eyes once haphazardly peered into mine with much sorrow.
Once our lives, full until love was buried beneath blankets of rage and broken promises,
perhaps would surface with the changing of the times.

Dark memories carried by the wind and dampened by the rain
Could open the skies, then disappear
As stardust glistening then fading into the twilight
Where your spirit once lost, would gracefully return…

Claudia A Krizay

Electroconvulsive Therapy

In this moment I feel as if I am falling,
Into a prison from nowhere,

I see my shadow arabesque
As my reflection appears
In a river of never abating madness-

Moments have passed since I lay upon
A cold metal table,
Drifting off to sleep,
chasing my dreams towards oblivion.

I am alive though within some obscure moment
Where I feel my heart rhythmically pounding
As is it were trying to escape
From a prison of impenetrable steel on death row.

My thoughts are spinning erratically
As would a horse upon a merry go round
It's motor rapidly accelerating.

As that horse bobs up and down
Exacerbating my fear-
I hear myself screaming
In the midst of a raucous silence.

I am climbing cliffs of cragged stone
Searching frantically beyond the skies
For a heaven of rapture and serenity,

As I surreptitiously open my eyes,
Ceiling lights become the rising sun.
I believe I have reached that paradise.

I fall into a tranquil river
Where skies of cerulean blue
Are sharply mirrored, allowing my reflection to flourish.

I swim to the bank of this river with utmost conviction,
Leaving the madness behind-

Claudia A Krizay

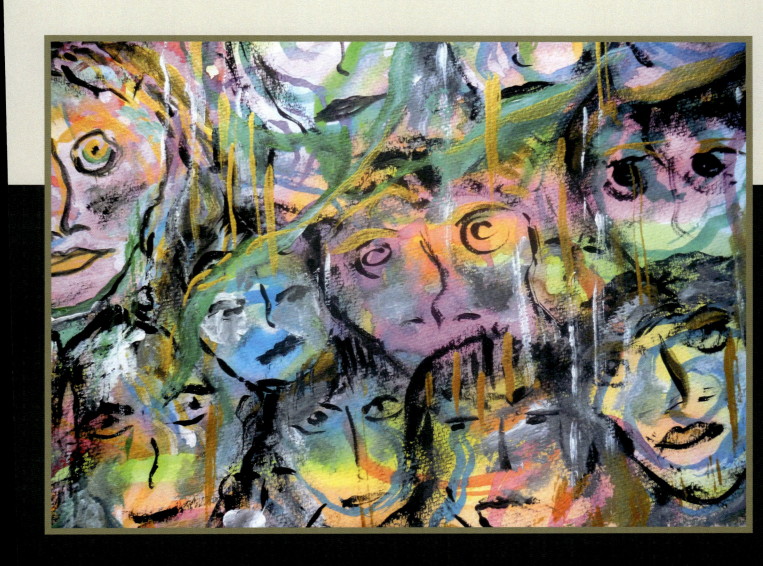

Empty Road

Living inside of this vast and populated world has been
As wandering upward an empty road without awareness.

Streetlights turn red whenever I wish
To move forward to pursue my dream.

False promises, hills, insurmountable, expectations never met-
I always remain gazing upward towards the sky,

I can foretell late summer's sultry thunderclouds and ravines in a distance-
I have travelled many an empty road before..

No matter how fruitful or tranquil a dream can be,
somehow it has always been interrupted by obscuring shadows,
or fissures into which I am falling and falling where no ground awaits me.

While merely existing outside of my own private world,
I do surmise that barricades can be removed,
Where ancient flowering trees can grow alongside-
Behind which I can hide though, momentarily.

I teeter upon the edge of that fine line that
That divides my dream space from all that is real.

I close my eyes to attempt once again
To follow my dream, now becoming an insurmountable hill in itself-

I have been told by a tremulous voice so very much alive
somewhere inside of the tenement of my mind
that I can overcome what seems impossible.

Streetlights never stay red for an eternity.
When cragged mountains begin to shatter
Perhaps within an avalanche, I know that I still must climb them-

When lies and broken promises that have plagued me every instant of my life
have been forgotten, I stand atop that snowcapped mountain peak
gazing upward towards galaxies trillions of light years away-

A surge of vigor races through my mind, unstoppable-
I know that even reality could someday be a dream coming to life-
I am wandering many empty roads but with more awareness.

Claudia A Krizay

Finding Myself

A lone sparrow I am,
Who could never fly high above dark and ominous clouds-
I swim an ocean that runs dry after a monsoon-
Only a dim reflection in a pond devoid of water-

I am a python locked inside of a barbed wire cage,
A barren tree struck by the force of a brutal storm…
My branches reach upward towards the skies
Like arms waving as in a cry for help-

Red ants are on fire crawling beneath my skin-
While my eyes spin about erratically as fractured dervishes-

The crescent moon wails cacophonously
While stars are fluttering like cinders as they near the ground-
Wires inside of my mind have become disconnected
Electrocuting my dreams?

Today I voyage upon a ship with silver sails
Riding tidal waves, invisible but viciously intensifying-
My silhouette is hardly visible in that pond devoid of water
I feel an intrinsic force seething within-
I am nowhere to be found.

I am soul searching, still navigating the ocean
Upon a ship with silver sails
While demons chatter with the red ants
Seething with rage beneath my skin.

I seek reason, and abandon false promises as I explore my dreams
Yearning for an exquisite sunrise
Casting fluorescent illumination over a world inside of which I am lost-
When I close my eyes the sun sets the galaxy afire.

When I open my eyes I see my shadow
Lingering about that pond devoid of water
Transforming to a clear reflection of the warrior I have become.
After cosmic rain has begun to fall…

Claudia A Krizay

Flights of My Imagination

A range of voices are summoning me
Where veracity is none but flight of my imagination

As the moon rises above purple mountains
I gather my strength into the core of my heart.
I erect wooden fences about me to safeguard my thoughts,
precious, though often complex and bewildering.

The moon seeks refuge behind silver- gray clouds overtaking the night
As I continue my solitary walk, towards majestic castles of my fondest reverie-
Sky lightening ignites the cosmos…

I continue my journey towards alluring silence-
I laugh at the humor of my plight- Raindrops spatter, though gently
upon the foundation that I walk-

My reflection glows in a nearby pond.
Scattered cirrus clouds have returned
Allowing sunlight to peer through- indiscreet-but almost spectacular.

Newfound illumination is constantly building rainbows,
Where wooden fences once prevailed.

Alien faces, commanding voices
And those majestic castles that exist beyond the clouds
Are peculiarly unique-
As they become none but reflections in a nearby pond-
Flights of my imagination…

Claudia A Krizay

Healing

Faces of terror appearing about mountains of madness,
Command me to ascend upward towards stark clouds of oblivion,

The many moons of Saturn
are conquered by asteroids imploding,
then reappearing below the graphite-hued sky above-

I stand alone within a remote celestial garden
Beneath a sky that has rained pulsars and quasars
Emanating from distant heavens.

Days of dismay, visions gone awry,
Moments of disharmonious thoughts and
Memories of a life defeated by torrential acidic rain dissipate
while fading into distant galaxies.

Meandering about cragged rocks destined to find serenity.
My shadow drifts into some distant stratosphere…
Where bold but scattered starlight has cleansed faces of terror-

The miracle of Saturn's enigmatic rings,
the viridian glow of Venus rising
and the crescent moon's remotely gleaming light
are revitalizing the bleakness of passing storm clouds.

Surrounded by the enticing and glorious flames
Emitted by far away galaxies light years away-
my soul emerges as a lone but vigilant star
visible from black holes of this universe.

Healing powers of illumination
have found strength and good fortune
While carrying my spirit to another realm.

After the moment in time
When all of the stars have burnt out,
Smoldering ashes shall consume faces of terror
As they vanish beyond collapsing mountains of madness.

Claudia A Krizay

Injection

I stumble over time as I venture outward,
dodging demons from distant galaxies, stalking me.
I shudder In a frigid mid-March breeze-

Trees are almost in full bloom-
Coming alive unknowingly- I break into a run.

Obstacles block the pathway upon which I wander.
Strange faces and unfamiliar glances
become most prominent- graphite hued skies
Attempt to inundate and overpower me.

I find myself soon to enter the very same room,
An hour later than the fortnight past,
Where an Asian nurse with hair dyed fire engine red,
Donning worn shoes of chartreuse patent leather-
Would greet me with her wan expression-

Stabbing me with a needle sharp as the sting
Of a yellow jacket – she injects me with some unique
And seemingly magical potion, mystifyingly healing-

Unfamiliar glances become more familiar now,
As wrathful voices are silencing.
I find comfort in my reveries- where insights have been rekindled.

Uncanny but soothing voices chant their garbled lullabies
While the sun attempts to break through darkened clouds of graphite and steel-

Skies are transforming to a rare shade of cyanotic blue,
As garbled voices dissolve into the stardust
Amongst which I am hiding.

Awareness is stirring as magenta and vibrant as sky lightning,
An amazing escape from madness-
Where these fleeting moments, now revitalized,
have become frighteningly clear….

Claudia A Krizay

Intergalactic Dance

Amidst a twilight interspersed with neon stardust,
Robed in a sateen scarf adorned with iridescent light
Tumultuous and vibrant bionic waves sweep over me
Belligerently as a lion's roar.

Journeying towards a new and unknown universe.
Neon stardust stirs a fire within my soul,
Encased within an opalescent glow.

The moons of Jupiter, Uranus and Neptune-
Are lightly shaded by the amazing rings of Saturn
And by the mysticism of what we have not yet been foretold.

Rhythmic music as played upon an orchestra drumming
Sets my spirit dancing with newly born asteroids
In a most amiable late night gathering.
A multitude of stars come out from hiding
To join in this intergalactic dance-

Neon stardust forms rainbows in the darkness
On this extraordinarily monumental night.
My aspiration has always been to become a star.

I dance about this cosmic horizon with grace and levity
Adorned with the iridescence of a flamboyant sateen scarf
Shadowing memories of bleaker nights and days.

Cloudbursts of neon stardust form rainbows over time
in a most unlikely but captivating way-
Past days that were phantoms in the darkness have been outshone
By the light of a most radiant star I have come to be….

Claudia A Krizay

Life in the land of the Dead 2

I was brought here into the land of the living dead-
Upon this pathway I take my walk alone.
My feet would hit the ground with hard and heavy steps.
I hear cymbals crashing inside of my mind and the tuneless sound of beating drums.
I have somehow lost myself along the way.

A tormented and weeping soul I am,
Drowning within a sea of shattered tranquility
Only my shadow, has silently slipped away
Through an open crack in the back door of this place,
This place where the carpet is chartreuse, and urine stained-
The stench of perspiration reeks here in this room,
And the tiled walls are sallow and filthy.

I sit upon this chair, its upholstery badly torn,-
Foam rubber poking out of every hole.
Old men, zombie-like- overly medicated,
Pace up and down these halls, along their pathway towards hell,
A pallid faced old woman stares into space-
Her wrists are bandaged- both of them-

I can hear the piano playing out of tune in the solarium
While my pounding heart cries out for some compassion-
I cry for help to come and rescue my dissolving spirit-
I am a captive inside of my own world,
Climbing invisible steps towards nowhere- inside of my worm-infested brain-

An Italian woman is screaming inside that room they call "seclusion"
That room where they had locked me into last night-kicking and screaming-
Now it is her turn to face the hopelessness of despair.

The bitter taste of liquid Thorazine lingers upon my tongue
Masked by the saccharine sweet taste of the donut I ate this morning,
I hear a young girl weeping bitterly
While an African woman whines out some unrecognizable tune-

This is the land of the living dead. I am locked inside this land of eternal death.
I cannot cope and I wish to harm myself.
Playing cards and broken chessmen are strewn about the floor, as
I listen to scratched records screeching upon the phonograph.

I hear strange voices- they want me to die.
Only I can hear them, so I am locked inside of this place.
This place-I call the land of the living dead.
Jarring bells are chiming as that decrepit ping pong ball rallies on.
I stuff torn sheets of newspaper hopelessly inside my ears
As I try to muffle the sound at night so that I can sleep??

This is the place they brought me to.
No one goes to heaven anymore- this place is lower than the hell beneath my feet.
Beat those drums slowly as my time, I believe, has come.
I keep pacing up and down these dimly lit halls alone.
Everybody shall die someday- my spirit I feel has already perished inside this dungeon.

As I keep walking backward and forward down these yellowed linoleum floors
I can see through a mist of tears that the gates of hell have opened to let me enter-
I am sinking into an endless gust of eternal fire.

Destined to be trapped here within this prison forever, I am.
It is five past one and I can almost hear a time bomb ticking.
I ride upon a suicidal roller coaster, every day and night.
I have little hope of reaching heaven anymore-
And I believe I shall never get a glimpse of the sunlight again-

I can still taste the bitterness of liquid Thorazine searing my tongue.
God has forsaken me, and I am locked inside of this vault.
My cries for help remain unheard. I shall never hear voices of angels singing,
This is my graveyard where hell has succumbed and taken over me

I pray for rain to put out the fire that burns my dissolving soul to ashes-
But only my tears are falling-
Because I can still hear the turning of the key within the lock,
The lock to that iron door which had been slammed behind me last night-
Past days are forever gone, and I cannot foretell the future.

I cannot see beyond these dingy yellowed walls.
I am none but a ghost and only angels sing in heaven.
I am trapped inside this lurid tomb and all I can see is darkness ahead-
I cannot hear angels singing and I cannot see the light of day-
No one can rescue me from my madness-

Claudia A Krizay

Locked Ward

As I amble down this dimly lit hallway perhaps a shadow would pass me by,
Or a warbler would chant in tune to a tranquil and truthful song
That emanates from the core of me

I would run with much agility upon a thoroughfare in the sky if I was able,
And lose myself inside of a world that is alive behind a rising star
As the evening transforms to a vibrant shade of cobalt blue.

The sun that has set behind me is casting shadows
That become as ghostly demons- reminiscent of
Days spent in a locked ward where there existed no recourse from fear.
Shadows are dreams that have become terrifying visions-
I can hear the distinct calling of the deceased
Emanating from beneath a slate-gray granite roadway paved before and behind me-

I recall a gale warning from years past
Where towering oak trees alive perhaps for thousands of years
Would lose their strength, become brittle and fall, and surround me,
As do the paint-chipped, sallow walls which are encompassing me now-
So far removed from a spark in a directing flame that could guide me towards
The exclusive paradise I had created in an attic room that no one believed existed.

Dim fluorescent lights shine with horror upon
Soiled and cracked tiled floors of this infernal tenement of dread and bewilderment
Where zombie-like beings pace behind and before me,
Their minds numbed by shock where everyone has become unrecognizable.

If I could find solace in fantasy as that which could be found in
My own back yard I believe I could survive inside of this purgatory-
I would follow the shadows that once were at a time soothing if I could…

As dusk settles, the faint light of the crescent moon outside
Casts obscuring silhouettes upon the walls
of these bleak cemented chambers of mayhem.
I vaguely recall ancient voices of my past, warning me to never look forward as
Gale warnings could recur and fallen trees would once again surround me.
I fear looking back as this world inside of my nightmares could last eternally-

I feel the force of strong and callused hands grasping my arms
and forcing me into a vapid cell where I am existing in the present,
listening to the faraway song of a warbler as it chants its peaceful lullabies….

Claudia A Krizay

Lover of Moon and Stars

(to my mother)

With utmost sorrow, I gaze into your eyes.
You lie still as a fallen birch tree after a winter's squall-
The demon that ravaged your mind
Has mercilessly robbed you of your sight.

When I was none but a child
You often read me enigmatic tales of the moon and stars,
That abundantly encircled our galaxy.

Once a worshipper of skies of cyanotic blue,
the skies inside of your darkened world
have been brutally overshadowed by an impervious fog.

I can still hear you chanting, backward in time
When the moon would gallantly reveal its countenance,
Surrounded by iridescent starlight.

Your spirit conveys an aura
That seems to emanate about the entire universe-
The moon rises at dusk
above violet hued mountains visible on every horizon.

If I could somehow create
a sudden and miraculous moment-
that dazzling starlight would break through the darkness,
and you would rise to the strength and power I know exists within you.

The miracle of stellar magic
Exists light years away,
While newly born stars are awaiting your vigilance
Not too far beyond astonishing skies of cyanotic blue…

Claudia A Krizay

Miracles

To foresee faces of terror
While climbing upward towards oblivion,
I could envision the spiritual splendor of Saturn cavorting
Amongst its many moons,
In miracles I do believe.

Surrounded by insurmountable cliffs, and
Drifting away into some foreign galaxy
I would awaken in my own celestial palace
In which I could dwell forever
In my dreams, I do believe....

An aura about the crescent moon intensifies
Guiding me away from facades
of my past nightmarish visions-
In hope, I do believe.

Beams of rainbow-hued enlightenment are soothing
and I hear a calling from beyond darkening cloud formations
telling me I have been chosen to save the souls of those who despair-
In my foremost delusions I had once believed.

Through raging tempests and ferocious windstorms
I am a survivor amongst downpours of toxic rain
That have fallen over the stillness of time.
In nature's temperaments I do believe..

I have been cleansed by the facets of my own imaginings-
I have survived storms and toxic rain
And battled faces of terror-
In my innermost strength I do believe-

I have escaped delusions of grandeur
And apparitional threats of persecution-
I dance with Saturn at nightfall
Amongst its many moons-
I do believe in myself.

Because I do believe in myself.
In miracles, I do believe.

Claudia A Krizay

Moments

Perhaps a shadow would pass me by,
Alongside the pathway I wander-

Japanese maple trees- in all of their crimson splendor
Shade me from the blaze of an early evening's sun-
I sense my spirit prospering.

I thrive inside of this realm
amidst cirrus clouds that embellish the sky.

Shadows could transform to moments-
Of a tranquil zephyr whispering
Within the litheness of splendor encompassing me.

My heart trembles amorously as
my fogged silhouette vanishes beyond myriads of towering birch trees.

Dewdrops settle like iridescent aventurine
upon flight of my imagination,
as cirrus clouds begin to dissipate,

My journey climaxes in the heavens —
Where islands of pearl-white sandstone glisten beneath frolicking stars.

Skies of azure-blue
are reflecting the holographic glow of Saturn's rings,

Amidst these rare and exquisite moments,
I see further than I can imagine

Claudia A Krizay

My Agile Spirit

My agile spirit
chants wondrous arias which soothe me as I dream.

The artist of my soul paints vibrant colors reflected by the rising of the moon
As it wanes with utmost promise past the midnight hours.

I travel towards unknown places beyond radiant silver cirrus clouds
That adorn the early morning's sunrise.

I explore the universe with my most adored companion,
the spirit that has prospered inside of me.
I have built a citadel from gilded visions where I jubilantly reside.

My citadel has been touched by
Muted colors of a rainbow Illuminating the pathway towards my dreams.
My dreams are of nature, and invincibility, where I stand firmly upon the element of pride.

I have created monoliths of platinum, capturing falling stars to embellish my horizon,
And have fabricated a throne built from self-acceptance and true devotion-

I can envision none but tranquility inside of this small world In which I dwell.
Here, enchanting visons of birch trees would appear
and wild roses are growing highly to explore life beyond the clouds.

Loneliness is fear, lurching in undesired solitude.
Those who are lonely amongst themselves
are lost souls trapped within the bleakness of despair.
It has been inscribed across the heavens that solitude
can become a rare and desirable treasure to behold.

My spirit chants solos which surround the sanctuary of my world
With their mystical intonations-
I dream of the moonrise and falling stars,
Peaceably, alone…

Claudia A Krizay

My Invincible Silhouette

I dance in rhythm with the changing of the seasons.
I become sky lightning as a storm approaches.
I fight with thunder in an approaching squall.

I rage war with the fury of the wind- With the locusts, I scream.
A creek's water rushes over its banks, and
As torrential rains inundate,
I have been revitalized as a silhouette reflected in an azure-blue pond.

Thunder claps. Dark clouds sigh.-
motionless, but vengeful.
I have become that silhouette, slumbering peaceably
As spirits of angels,
Tenderly chant amidst their dwellings beyond the skies.

My silhouette is silent as the clouds,
Cautiously gazing upwards towards the heavens
dreaming of galactic nights and rainbows to be reborn at every sunrise.

I am a shadow-like being that blends with the darkness.
As Venus rises
I have become that silhouette that reappears, then rises into its power,
Once abandoned and somewhat bewildered.

As a hauntingly alluring silhouette
I blend with shadows of growing trees, then fading into the night-
As shy as a fawn, but boldly invincible,
I scream with the locusts, then sing with the mellow tones of starlings.

As a transcendent silhouette, I disappear
into a mountain of clouds as I return to my power,
courageous, and serenely vigilant.

Lost somewhere in these ominous clouds, I foresee a safe haven-
As my spirit dissolves into nothingness.

Claudia A Krizay

My Only Veracity

I lose myself within this place of my visions,
this land of nowhere- my only veracity.

My world has a name which I cannot reveal.
Each person whom I converse with also has a name-
My closest companion always present
connects with me through her eyes of cyanotic blue.

I can see her flaxen hair tossed about in
A rare breeze that only drifts inside my world, untouched by fire-
This world, so pure, harmonious, and always tranquil…

Cacophonous sounds echo from the outside of the gate that has been padlocked
To bar others from entering the land of my visions- my only veracity-
That world with a name I cannot reveal to those who reside where darkness prevails.

I have been reborn inside of a world. where unicorns roam plentifully
while rainbows are dancing- -stars shine vibrantly at the noon of the day,
And the sunlight illuminates my dreams close to the midnight hours.

I ride bareback upon a unicorn prancing through a hazy mist
Of iridescent stardust against that rare breeze
That only exists inside of my world untouched by demons of my past.

I capture the moonlight amongst my illusions within a sapphire net
And release it towards the heavens-

I strum my unique and mystical harp and chant melodious tunes
Of sincere love for my adored companion-
as she gazes at me through her eyes of cyanotic blue.

My father would tell me many tales- tales of truth of the world outside,
where boisterous crowds linger, dancing to the rhythm of erratic drumming,
wars are raging, and rain falls in torrents- and that we cannot escape what is real-

My reality has become this place of my visons,
This land of nowhere, this extraordinary place
where sunlight is unveiled at the midnight hour-

I have lost myself with deep gratitude to this incredible place which has
a very special name that I cannot ever reveal-
this land of nobody is my only veracity…

Claudia A Krizay

49

Never Believe What is Real

Set fire to my soul
And burn in cold blood.
Listen to the voices commanding-
And always obey.

Fear intensifies at the moment
The risen sun robs you of all of your might.
All I can foresee are shades of iridescent green.

While Venus is rising,
Fond memories execute.
I can feel the agony of oblivion.

Magenta orchards
emanate from the skies- bearing magical fruit.
I have never believed what is real.

Light is darkness.
I can see beyond these conniving eyes.

Have you ever witnessed Mars
Turning crimson behind the rising moon
When all of the stars have frozen?

We have planted seeds of redemption,
While raindrops are sprouting
From high grasses that are touching the skies.

We are gliding through the wind
Upon oceans of madness.
Light is blackening.

Life is a resurrection
When we open our thoughts
Towards the skies after a squall.

Even after dying thoughts have resounded,
I have never believed what is real.

Claudia A Krizay

Present Moment

There must be a paradise that awaits me-
Today I am destined to search- I must keep on believing
there exists a special haven for me to reside.

Here in this place silver roses and aromatic carnations
Would blossom within a fantasy coming to life.

I hope for a magical space in time
when forsythias would flourish above high grasses-
Their golden petals fluttering in a placid spring's zephyr.

I dream of cavorting amongst peonies and marigolds
Across a field as vast as our infinite universe
before that day my spirit would escape me.

I foresee a day or perhaps a starlit evening
When my spirit shall prosper as would vines of ivy
Climbing upward the rugged trunk of the tallest maple tree.

I shall collect the supple petals of wild violets within my cupped hands
As they flurry about in a gust of wind.
I would chase dandelion thistles until they fade into the sunrise
Enamored of the mysticism of their fragility-

Encircled by Japanese maple trees, hydrangeas,
And ever so rare lilies of the valley-
their delicate scents would permeate my surroundings-

No one knows precisely where their pathways lead towards,
After their souls and spirits evade them-
I find myself stumbling upon that mesmerizing moment in time.

I hear the distant cry of a nightbird in flight above evergreen trees of fortune,
Welcoming my spirit homeward-
That spirit that may never evade me-

Claudia A Krizay

Rainbow Dancing

I may have seen a rainbow dancing
Rising above the clouds, crimson, and vermillion in their hues.
Darkness lifts the light away
Upon the essence of time.

Alien faces are frighteningly threatening, as
Souls are rising from the deceased-
Spirits lost in the depth of the forest
indulge in profound conversation.

I am grasping at my thoughts, vaguely conflicting-
I can hear chattering voices, blindly emanating from ghostly intruders-

As a reflecting pond captures frozen dewdrops,
Unfamiliar glances are becoming suspiciously terrifying.
I peer through barren tree branches.
As I journey towards that wondrously enticing oblivion-

Freezing rain spatters, though gently upon the pathway that I walk-
I see my reflection wading in a nearby creek,
Crimson and vermillion clouds are rising once again
Lightly glazed with gilded stardust-

I can foresee that rainbow dancing
Amongst silencing threatening voices-
The darkness has been furtively stolen
By a sorcerer of the night…

Claudia A Krizay

Seed

Once a seed, born near a ravaging creek
Shaded by blossoming hyacinths,
Fed by night terrors of years past-
I was consoled by the enchanting songs of sparrows…

I would surmise, then wonder
If I had lost control of time,
And compliance with the world outside…

My spirit has blossomed
Amongst trees sustaining lives for perhaps a millennium.
Hidden beneath stones polished by waters of rushing streams
I was once invisible to the world surrounding…

I feared growing tall to meet with storm clouds,
To be consumed as if by vultures,
And the loss of control of my existence-
Rudely snatched away by the wind, I would weep dewdrop tears…

Alone amongst high grasses, overpowered,
And terrified of losing the grounds into which I was born,
I shivered, then shuddered amidst a relentless spring's snowstorm.

Seizing my power I prosper to become a sapling,
Exquisite, and robust while dancing
Amongst long stemmed and fragrant carnations-

My leaves, adorned with silver stardust,
stunningly robed in sunlight at every dawning
And capturing the moonlight past the midnight's hours,
I find myself no longer terrified of nature's guiles…

I flourish as a tree amongst many, young but thriving.
Fears of terrors of the night and high winds
Have transformed to none but shadows.

A seed remaining near a ravaging creek,
Shaded by blossoming hyacinths-
Shall someday grow to dance amongst long stemmed carnations,
Robust and proud to be embracing the skies…

Claudia A Krizay

Silver Rose

When I close my eyes to the world outside.
I believe I can find a rare and magnificent silver rose,
very much alive in all of its wondrous glory.

I can recall many regally enchanting roses growing in my father's garden.
I can still hear his faltering footfalls resounding from his new home amongst the skies,
Decades after his passing.

Bleak darkness reigns,-though when I close my eyes I can still see roses-
yellow, red, and those uniquely silver-toned,
their supple petals reflecting both doleful and jubilant memories.

Although a stranger to this world
And now a stranger alone in what was once my father's sanctuary,
I can see copious silver roses thriving amidst their thorny stems,
swaying in a raucous winter's breeze.

Upon this extraordinary winter's night –
stars are gleaming from within their iridescent shadows
Illuminating this now barren space-

Roses of yellow and red, now vanishing and dissipating
Had once been scenic and fragrant- always blossoming-
.
Silver roses are still miraculously and clearly flourishing,
As the others have withered and have been scattered about the ground to perish.

Darkness prevails but I believe I see one remaining star
Vibrantly glistening on this sharply frigid midwinter's night.

This unique star, reflecting a lone and alluring silver rose,
appears irrevocably striking- beneath the illumination of distant galaxies.

Perhaps my father's spirit is alive and prospering within that mystical silver rose,
rising from amidst the darkness-
Where a night has never appeared so bountiful and majestic.

Claudia A Krizay

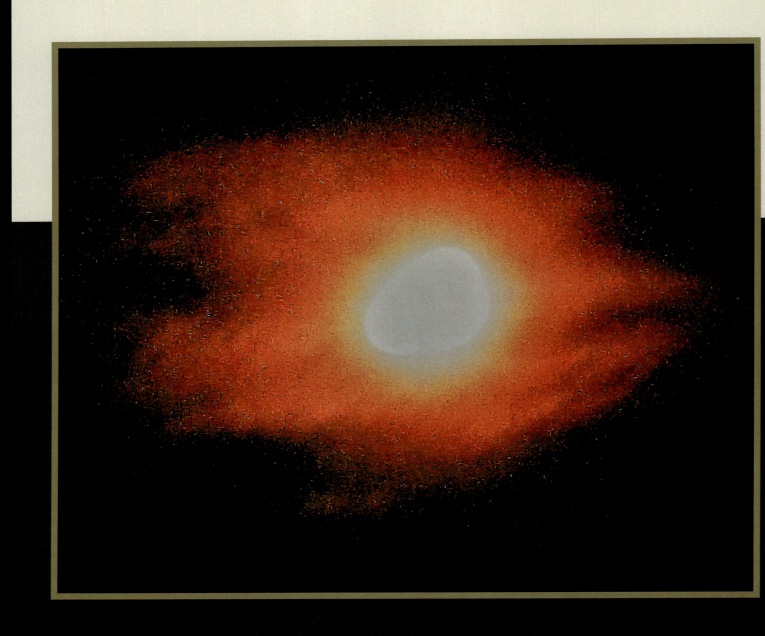

Surviving

My mother used to tell me that I am angry at the world.
My mother has left this world.

I remember the night my father
Pulled me from the bathtub and threw me on the floor,
And beat me with his iron studded belt- I began
To scream in pain- he left me there in a heap to cry and
My mother did not comfort me.
My father has left this world.

I am angry at the world, where people roam everywhere.
I have no safe haven outside these doors- my only refuge is the world
Inside of my mind- voices that speak inside of my mind
Are my closest friends and the people that roam the streets outside
Are my demons- they chatter like cackling chickens on their phones
And I wonder, are they talking about me? Or are they trying to disturb me?

They talk of me, and they disturb me- I remember my mother in this moment-
My mother has left this world.
I find fleeting comfort in the thought that she is looking down upon me.
But her eyes, radiating disbelief are burning me like the toxic rays of the risen sun
Or burning my soul with stardust on fire past the midnight hours

Upon this sleepless night where all I can see are pythons crawling upon my bedside
Or an angry demon dumping rats upon the dusty carpet of my
dilapidated room? My mother does not comfort me. My mother is self-absorbed-

My mother long ago has left this world. She left this world before she passed away.
She entered the dark chambers of depression, and my father assigned me to be her keeper.
In books they call it "suicide watch."
My father has left this world.

Black skies and foggy mornings dominate this world- I am journeying forward daily
Trying to find myself. I have been left behind. I cannot find my way outside this world.
I am locked inside of a loop of toxic rain-my tears drown my spirit-

I do not know myself. But I have known abuse. I have known rage and sorrow.
I have not known tranquility or safety. I am angry at this world. Children are screaming and
car alarms are sounding. Noise is torture and god has forsaken me and shall not stop
Cacophonous sounds that are tearing my soul to pieces?

My grandmother believed in God, heaven, and angels. My grandmother has left this world. Will
I go to heaven when I leave this world? Does anyone go to heaven anymore? They say my mother
and father are living in a better place? I shall try to climb that ladder towards heaven.

The rungs upon that ladder shall break or I shall reach the top and my
mother and my father shall be awaiting my arrival.
My father shall greet me with a whip and my mother, with her histrionic ways.
My grandmother, with her ludicrous stories of heaven and hell.

So blessed I am, I hear others say I was struck with such fortune to have led a great life with such amazing
parents- nobody saw them when their eyes were closed. Nobody can see them when their eyes are wide open.
But I can see them when my eyes are closed. I can see them when my eyes are open.
I see them everywhere.

I am angry at the world. I disdain humanity. I only love myself. My mother has left this world.
My father has left this world. The skies rain ammonia that sears my flesh. My skin crawls. Snakes
constrict my mother's severed arm. She has never left the world inside of my diseased brain where I
cry out from the confinements of a locked ward- enclosed inside of a room they call "seclusion".

As would a brave, but wounded eagle I lift my damaged wings and fly.
Soaring high above magenta clouds and violet mountains,
I rise to my inner strength and power..

Claudia A Krizay

Tears

Tears are fierce as summer rain- tears are toxic when wept with anger.
Tears are sordid memories. Tears are threats of suicide.

Tears are frightening as sky lightening.. Tears can be audible- my mother weeping
alone In her room downstairs. My tears are cried with pain, and empathy.

Tears are faucets of tepid water that drowned me after my father hurt me.
My tears are invisible. My tears are audible.

Tears are ice storms that surge when loved ones die. Tears are blood that frightens children.
Tears embarrass when people weep for foolish reasons.

Tears are panic when I lose hope. Tears are frantic when I lose my mind.
When I lose my mind, my tears are cragged rocks that irately tumble from the heavens.

Tears are shattered glass- Tears cried from broken promises.
Tears con people to forgive and forget.

Tears can be a desperate cry for help Tears are cleansing,
And can be amazing as meteors showering from the twilight's skies

Tears emanate from a tremulous heart. Or tears can be our spirit's joy.
Tears can inundate like a tidal wave that carry me away from reality.

Tears fill an aquarium that can overflow..
Tears are wrong doings that arouse ridicule- tears are mocking.

Some say tears are signs of cowardice. those who cry tears from the sincerity of their hearts
are brave and strong as hard-edged steel.. Tears are honest-

Tears are lilacs, flamboyant in a tranquil breeze.

Claudia A Krizay

Ten Steps

Conniving eyes envelop me.
I bathe within a pool of molten lava- One of my foremost nightmares.

I take ten steps downward towards hell.
This basement is my inferno where I wade in sultry cinders.

My pupils spin as they meet eye to eye with Satan's-
my father's piercing stare-he rants discordantly.

My father is my predator-one of many,
As one in a hungry pride of lions, destined to kill.

Walls are painted crimson red. I meet face to face with bedlam.
The ceiling collapses into a downpour of disarray.

Fire rages in every corner-
Tepid water splashes upon the concrete floors.
Smoke rises- my father's raging violence.

Lakes of anguish are seething-
My father, possessed by demons.

I recall my late mother's words:
"Someday you shall find your safe haven."
I take ten steps upward, searching-

My pupils meet with the angry eyes of God-
my deceased father's wicked countenance.

The skies rain ashes- the heated wrath of God.
Relief from utter dread is lost inside of bleak storm clouds of oblivion.

I have taken ten steps upwards,
After confronting the gates of purgatory-

in a distance, I foresee my father's ghost
wading through sultry cinders, dispersing into the night.
Where I have found my safe haven…

Claudia A Krizay

The Bus Ride

I disdain your cacophonous laughter
And your unrelenting stares.
Move back further, and further away, as you enter,
Beyond my line of vision

I hear your scornful laughter-
I seek revenge.
I want to take this bus for a joyride
towards hell's eternal damnation.

You are standing before the yellow line-
Let the breaks slam!
Collide into the windshield and
Fall into the gutter amidst shards of glass and die.

Blood and guts are tangled beneath the wheels-
I am laughing with delight-
It serves you all right-

Insufferable demons,
You bear souls, possessed.
Police are searching for your wretched souls,
beneath the wheels of this bus.

I hear shouting and depraved laughter.
That echoes about- further, and further away….

A lone and threatening voice
emanates from a dented cell phone
lying upon the floor of this bus-
intermingling with the wrathful voices
that play havoc inside of my mind.

In my dreams I longed for this to happen-
While laughter and foreign tongues
echo about, the confinement of my mind.

I exit this inferno,
And stealthily walk the streets-
beyond your line of vision…
further, further, and further away…

Claudia A Krizay

The Geranium Plant

Geraniums are blossoming from a cracked clay pot, casting their slowly fading shadows,
About the worn and dusty carpet-
Your voice echoes about my mind-though you are no longer present—
I still hear you chanting your bittersweet arias
Somehow harmonious and uniquely mesmerizing.

Pictures upon your wall are fading- paint chips are falling from the ceiling
To randomly decorate the threadbare carpet-
Some higher being so rudely captured you as you were drowning in your sorrows-
The silence that reigns about this room, is so frighteningly deafening…

Wrinkled bedclothes are tossed upon the foot of your unmade bed.
Your shoes unlaced and silken scarf lie forlornly upon the floor.
Was it truly you who took your life,
Or was your soul whisked away by some evil ghostly sorcerer?

Tears emanate from my heart that bleeds remorse-
Your rare moments of laughter were special ones,
As was your pure love for the gifts of nature-
Fond memories I shall always contain within…

Every crimson petal that grows
From the blossoms of that geranium plant sadly reflects your mournful countenance-
And your lithe and fragile spirit- That spirit I hope shall soon be dancing with seraphs
In some brighter, and not too faraway place…

I hear rain falling now- each droplet tap dances upon the foggy windowpane.
Perhaps your tears are emanating from beyond darkening clouds of sorrow?
If I could, with some elusive optimism,
I would dance with you in that not too faraway place- and bring you back home to me…

Memories of you shall not rinse away the anger or the agony of loss,
But any abundance of tears shall never rinse away fond memories
Or the heartfelt passion for the distinctive spirit that you left behind…

The stems of the geranium plant have grown, reminiscent of your captivating spirit.
its strikingly crimson petals that flutter from every blossom
Still bearing your reflection- have been scattered in a gentle breeze,
While they remain untouched and uniquely mesmerizing….

Claudia A Krizay

The Mesmerizing Land of Itmon

My bed has become a ferryboat guiding me through the bleakness of
My sordid nightmares
Towards this mesmerizing world deemed as Itmon-

I am alive inside this faraway place, although
Truly not so far away-
The voices inside of my mind, commanding-
Giving me orders day in and day out-
My closest companions whose orders
I feel inclined to obey-

Running far away from the voices of my past where
This planet earth has not been kind-
The land of Itmon is none but paradise-

Here I have come to know Kyt, my guiding light
Donning flaxen hair and eyes of
Cyanotic blue-

Hypnotizing me with her glance and
Charming me with her smile,
She would take me by the hand and lead me towards
This magical land of Itmon-
This place where nobody feels despair
And where we lose ourselves within our dreams-

Pink clouds are turning lavender at night fall-
Snow never falls in this land of my fantasies-
Fantasies have so abruptly transformed to reality-

Hand in hand Kyt and I have abandoned the demons of
Our pasts and we have entered this place
Of our wildest dreams to remain forever bonded-

As an inhabitant of this planet I was so rudely born into,
I mounted my proud stallion and fled into the sunrise-
Then dismounting when I reached that path paved before me-
That path paved in platinum, which by nature has guided me
Towards the magnificent land of Itmon-

I see mountains of many colors-
Before whirlpools of waters of deep cobalt blue-
I stand stalwart besides tall reeds, viridian hued-
I am very much alive in this unique place of my dreams which
Has rapidly become my only reality-

Sing with me, Kyt, the song of a nightingale- for
I hear faint words of alien people saying that
I have lost my sanity and my mind is in a wretched state-
However, I have never been a happier person alive-
I have lost myself inside the world of my dreams forever-

My dreams are reality and yesterday's reality has vanished-
Looking into those eyes of Kyt's-
Compelling and hypnotic as in my fondest dreams-
Eyes of cyanotic blue- truly spellbinding, reflecting the daylight's shadows.

I have found a home that only I can envision-
Where I sit on the right side of the holy octagon and
Thank the Goddess that rules this fine land for
Making my dreams come alive-
My fantasies are my only true reality now.

Claudia A Krizay

Mysticism of My Spirit

My spirit, valiant and alive looks upward towards the sky,
Perhaps to someday awaken in another realm-
Alive, untouched, and unafraid,

Stars boldly contrast as would faceted crystals against the midnight's sky,
Far away, though nearby in quite a unique way-

Transforming to a gilded- feathered eagle
Upward I would soar
as my spirit attentively watches over me-

That spirit that dwells within-
has always been a force, brave, wise- and very much aware.

My spirit is my hope and my redemption
From the apparition of the nightmares of my past-

I follow in the footfalls of every direction
That my spirit proudly takes-
Enlightened by the mysticism of the rings of Saturn
And by the many moons of Jupiter.

My spirit sprightly dances-
vibrant as a newly born asteroid
transmitting its firing illumination
about every primeval galaxy-
But woefully lost within the azure-blue vastness of the universe.

I would fly upward as that gilded-feathered eagle
Always searching for that opaline fire ablaze within my spirit rising,
While abandoning my fears.

Perhaps someday my spirit shall reawaken
In some other realm-
Alive, unscathed, and unafraid,
Prudently watching over me…

Claudia A Krizay

The Truth of Living

At twilight, I rise to my omnipotence.
Dancing amidst the cosmos-

As I gaze upward towards autumn's skies I see the stars emerging.
An opalescent fog settles atop the full moon as I slumber.

In my dreams I carry my thoughts towards the spirituality of the universe-
My illuminated shadow fades into a magnificent, intergalactic moment-

As would a gull with wings of polished platinum
I soar, reflecting the rhythm of pulsating, distant stars.

Dreams are fleeting- I awaken,
As I open my eyes, I am blinded by the aura of the rising sun.

I close my eyes, delving back into fantasy
Where I find myself captivated by magenta and mauve cloud formations
That encircles my private tenement beyond distant skies.

Upon awakening, my dreams become delusions of my fondest desires,
waiting to come to life.

I waltz about groves of carnations in all of their carnelian glory-
Their delicate fragrance permeates the splendor of my shrouded world.

An approaching storm stirs my imagination
From which I once more arouse- dreams are fleeting.

Blustery winds in a mighty storm carry shimmering raindrops
Which cleanse the air that I breathe- birthing fields of lilacs, marigolds, and peonies -

These rare moments are becoming authentic-
distinctly rewarding- and joyfully everlasting.

Claudia A Krizay

They

(To the people inside of my mind)

They greet me every morning,
Often commanding,
At times, intrusive, conniving-
garbled and cacophonous-
transforming to a melodic whisper,
Though out of tune with reality…

Often present when I open my eyes
To a world, unreachable, foreign, and threatening…
They follow every footfall,
Often amusing, while at times invasive,
Returning in the night…
As gentle, and welcoming.

At times, aggressive, loudening, and menacing,
As a child I would listen amidst the darkness-
And often heard them calling-
I could see them, as terrifying,
And at times, picturesque, iridescent-
Almost amazing…

Upon awakening, they diminish,
Becoming almost inaudible-
I speak back to them wrathfully,
And at times, amicably,

They sharply louden and endanger,
As a tree falling in a storm,
Hitting the ground as in a raucous explosion…

Often horrific, at times inescapable,
My most derided enemies,
They become hostile, though bizarrely hospitable-

They are my most adored, attentive,
And constant companions,
melodically whispering,
out of tune with reality….

Thoughts Resonate

Trees bow to the rhythm of falling stars
Before and after this world was born-

Too many years have passed, and clouds have turned chartreuse in hue.
With freedom on the rise and the dogged determination of lost souls
perhaps we can recapture the stars-

Only the morning glories and evergreens are visible now-
I had believed that I owned the woodlands-
It has been said that too many tears have been wept for yesteryear-

Trees have been uprooted and tenements
of concrete, brick and stone have been built, adorned with crystalline highlights,
While I have only cared- about the deer, the lakes,
the distinct calling of a whippoorwill, and capturing those falling stars…

Tomorrow may be doomsday.
I shall lock every door that may lead to that place in time-
where all that remains would be
Stems and tree branches fallen- into a puddle of massive confusion-

Disdain for humanity has set fire to my spirit- though still on the run-
I have seized every thought within that needs to be heard
And captured each inside a fine net of woven silver threads.

Music resonates from faraway places.
I hear muted thunder emanating from glowing clouds of prosperity-
Perhaps a calling from distant heavens?

Walk through this forest of life-that life which belongs only to you-
Even after the stars have fallen and disappeared.

Slowly walk and follow your lead-
Grasp every thought and mold it into fortune.
Thoughts become majestic when they have been unfurled
And could become gifts for prospects to flourish-

Trees bow to the rhythm of a gentle breeze
In this special moment where this world has been reborn…

Claudia A Krizay

Thoughts

My thoughts are so like impervious thunderclouds
Only welcoming the light of my inner spirit to shine though
- when lightening has struck inside of my mind-

I ride my phantasmal though legendary stallion into the night
Where skies are never clear and shaded by magenta clouds, so enticing,

Deep azure blue is the color of the universe-
Dank as the clouds before an intergalactic storm.
Our thoughts become synchronized with every color of a rainbow
Illuminated by a flash of sky lightening- or amidst a vicious meteor shower.

As that rainbow dissolves into the cosmos,
a melodious sonatina rings throughout the universe-
Our thoughts become like impervious thunderclouds.

Claudia A Krizay

Too Many Dreams

Drawings and cut- out figures
Had always been most prominent
Trapped inside of my childlike spirit

I had secured that wrought iron gate towards humanity-
When I was none but a child-
threatened by too many dreams-

Diamond headed snakes would writhe about my bedside,
or harmless, iridescent helium balloons would hover
near the ceiling in the darkness of the midnight hours-
My delusional world-

When the night was barely alive,
And the mornings, unrecognizable
I would find myself gazing with caution beyond the boundary of time.

Locked inside of a cloud-like vault with an apparitional sterling key
I would build a life of cut out figures- each having a name-
They became my angels from a different galaxy, or perhaps
Some other universe-

Barricaded inside of this world
I had fabricated for myself alone-
I would laugh and play harmless but juvenile games
With these enchanting cut-out figures.

With a blunt pair of scissors
I would cut out angels with uneven paper wings,
Uniquely captivating and never menacing,

They would soar towards the ceiling, in all of their dazzling triumph,
To dance and chant amongst those fictitious helium balloons-
Calming me until I drifted into a restful slumber.

As a child of ten- I scarcely knew what was real-
though it hardly mattered- as this incredible cut -out world belonged to me, alone…

Claudia A Krizay

Tranquil World

Nobody has ever walked this path before-
Towards a tranquil world where only deer roam and birds take flight-
Nightingales, whippoorwills, and sometimes invisible angels
singing in harmony with songs of starlings
while cicadas would chant eerily, but melodiously-

I would safely hide behind a tall oak tree,
Where blue jays, hummingbirds and cicadas form a murmuring though distinctive choir,
Chanting the verses of the songs my mind composes,
In a rare and clairvoyant manner.

Nobody has ever walked this path before,
This path to which I could journey to a paranormal world-
This magnificent world of my creation.
one so different and yet so unsettling,
as my surroundings could evade me within a sudden breath of wind…

I am singing my own songs pleasingly
Far away from menacing, outside intruders-
I shall have abandoned the nightmares of reality,
Reaching upward to touch some extraordinary stratosphere above the clouds
Though perhaps only in my dreams….

Conceivably I could be lost inside my own mystical reverie,
From which I care to never awaken.
I sing my own songs- hymns of passion of my most profound desires.

It hardly matters if they are none but apparitional-
As an artist, I believe I can create the perfect world of my fondest visions-
A painting that shall never fade even amidst the most radiant starlight.

Whether in wakefulness or within my deepest slumber,
There is so much inside my world to explore
Upon this pathway where nobody has ever walked before…

Claudia A Krizay

Unfamiliar World

I was born into an unfamiliar world
Walking through a steel and iron fogginess-
Dark, but eerily beautiful.

Somehow sky lightening or a stellar implosion
Though blinding, would capture my dreams
And magically transform them to a more tangible state of reality.

A different sort of sun shall rise
shining light upon my kaleidoscopic world-
Black skies transform to azure hues
As a hurricane of sorts shall carry sinister clouds away-

The moon in its obscure but profound glory
Shall rise above endless waterfalls
cleansing an uphill road, mysterious, though enticing.
Where alien voices shall be silenced-

I foresee a river rapidly receding then suddenly overflowing,
clear and opalescent, washing over me.
It was in that rare and terrifying instant
That I could see those dismal clouds returning-

Feelings are so like thunderclouds-
when sky lightening has struck your mind,
And callous feelings of rage return to haunt you.

Sensations of fear are staggering
Upon the border of castles built of sand and ocean waves-

Skies of Prussian blue so magnificent appear whenever I close my eyes-
While streaks of spectral moonlight shall someday decorate the skies
above this unfamiliar world into which I was conceived.

When stark clouds of steel and iron permeate the skies-
They shall become in many ways, distinctively mesmerizing.

The rising sun and other mystical celestial bodies
Shall illuminate the darkness and cast about muted hues of tranquility.

Soundless waterfalls cleanse lost and wounded spirits
restoring a world, serene and invitingly more familiar…

Claudia A Krizay

Vault

An iron vault is locked, containing gold and silver treasures,
Family photographs, poignant letters,
Reminiscent of times past and memories of distressing feelings
Never to be forgotten.

The details of my childhood's pain, and feelings of anger and fear
Are ever present, waiting to escape that iron vault,
As these thoughts and sordid memories have never been silenced.

My heart holds within feelings of betrayal,
Rage and suspicion and disdain for the world outside.

With every palpitation, I would wonder why so many trees have fallen,
Where the stars are hiding and recollections of the moment I became a lone gull
Spreading my wings to soar above violet-hued mountain peaks?

My mind is an impenetrable vault inside of which I have chosen to
Hold within consoling lullabies, visons of magenta and mauve cirrus clouds
That decorate my world- while rainbows are drifting beyond my horizon.

Alluring visions of silver roses reflect the early rising of the sun
Over deepening oceans of aquamarine…

My dreams are held within my mind, my heart, and my spirit, reborn-
Mistrust and fear are the keys that lock my spirit within, that yearn for freedom and
The desire to be understood-

Rain falling in torrents forms reflecting ponds where I can envision my shadow dancing,
Atop a violet mountain peak where I can see my world in all of its amazing glory.

Magically, every vault becomes unlocked with a gilded key of fortune,
Allowing years of pent up feelings of despair, rage, and fear to be carried away
To a realm beyond which I can foresee-

Magenta and mauve cirrus clouds linger about my dream space,
And silver roses are emerging in groves over time while I chant consoling lullabies-

I open my heart, my mind, and my spirit upon this triumphant moment in time
Where my dreams have escaped confining vaults
and have miraculously become my memorable and true reality.…

Claudia A Krizay

View from Seclusion at Sibley Hospital

Hypnotized by anesthesia- the bleakness of this room has overshadowed the risen sun.
Indulging in rare conversation with companions who are always with me-
Blind to the world outside- What I hardly remember Is now forgotten-

What I do recall I hope shall carry me homeward towards the place I had often dreamed of-
Though rudely interrupted by merciless shouting, amidst early morning hours-

The picture window I stand before Is a mirror to the outside world
where homes I can envision across the river are built upon a hillside-
I indulge in fantasies coming to life-

My dream space is summoning me home as I am sailing my dingy across the reservoir-
Visions of many colors- reflect hues of the daylight hours-

Skies of cerulean blue decorated by high cumulous clouds,
Interspersed with moments of haziness, tints of magenta touched with patches
Of light orange and crimson- Cloud formations from heavens of fortune
Are painting rainbows and waterfalls that surround this magical hillside-

Shadows of birch trees create enchanting formations-
Iridescent rainbows are reflecting in tranquil waters-The river's muted current carries my dreams
to a place beyond veracity as I weep tears of destitute realization.

Light is darkness- fantasy has become my only reality where I lose myself within a nirvana
That shall dissipate within the moment that I exit this room.

This chamber has become the stage where I have choreographed a wordless orchestra
Humming In tune with the incongruous but melodic chanting of robins, starlings, and orioles-
Outside of this extraordinary picture window.

I can see as clearly, as the day could become where I am residing in a phantasmal palace
Upon a hill viewing my silhouette as reflected within the serene waters of the reservoir-
To envision a dream coming to life Is admiring a scenic painting of how I believe this world should be-
Etched across a picture window- delights my imagination-

Shock had run rampant through my brain at the break of this day -
I see reality through a fog though still painfully clear-
I am locked inside of a charnel house where everyone is emotionally dying-

Claudia A Krizay

When I Cannot Sleep

When I cannot sleep
I hear distant voices summoning me
From some obscure place, unknown.

When I awaken from a restless slumber
Peculiar voices resonate.

I drop a tarnished silver coin
In a nonexistent creek,
Wishing upon a star,
Too far removed to fathom.

When I cannot sleep,
Strange voices echo about sallow colored walls,
Recreating memories of saddened earlier days.

I pray to a god, not certain of its existence.
I hide behind an iron monolith
Standing in its fortitude
amidst a land of nowhere.

I speak to people from a distant past,
Or to those whom I have fabricated.
When I cannot sleep,
I wish the surrounding world away.

When I lie awake strange beings appear to be harming me.
As I sleep, I am accosted by imaginary demons.

One day I shall find myself in limbo
Caught between sleep and wakefulness-
A safer place where I can thrive alone…

In a trance I count exquisite celestial bodies not too far above me-
As I dance about clearing skies and silent waterfalls.

Claudia A Krizay

Winter's Blossoms

Cherry trees do not blossom in the month of January.
I cannot dance in the midst of fire, and not get burned-
Aspirations have become shattered visions-

I cannot build monoliths that scrape the skies
I cannot break down these lurid walls that confine me
I cannot rise from the downtrodden
Or rebuild collapsed foundations from granules of quicksand.

I cannot stand tall amongst turbulent moments-
Or to quench the flames that sear my visons for a future
I cannot fathom finding respite in this irrevocable world
While I falter in every step I take towards emancipation from fear

I cannot lift my wings as would a monarch butterfly
Soaring above cirrus clouds against a sky of cerulean blue,
Whistling harmonious tunes amongst a discordant choir of angels,
While hiding behind the full moon past the deep dark hours of an eerie night.

I cannot speak to the world of the voices that only I can hear-
Or trust another with the code that opens my mind to those who wish me harm.
I can escape a maddening crowd with limbs that leap over cragged rocks
As would a wild cat on the run searching for its prey.

I can feel the pain of ridicule and the horrors of delusiveness
And I can speak to those who have made a home inside of the depths of my inner spirit.
So many dreams for renowned success have been buried
beneath the subzero temperatures of the thin ice of a glacier
where I have so often slipped and fallen through.

I can see through the darkness of my window of pain-
All of the dreams that have been carried away by tumultuous ocean waves-
The countless foundations I have created from the day I was born into this world
That erratically spins backward in time- have avalanched into an ice-clad valley-

I do believe there is no shame
in wishing for roses to blossom in the midst of winter-

Claudia A Krizay

You Dance Alone

There exists a world outside-
I could guide you down its pathway
Away from your fabricated heaven-

So much to see and so much to be heard-
To be amongst others and amidst gifts of nature
Where there are roads to walk forward in the cooling rain
or beneath the glorious light of the rising sun

There is a world out there- although you never cared.
You are locked inside a world of your creation,
Crying out to those who wish you harm,
Speaking to the voices only you can hear,
Watching the sun set- though in your world,
The moon is coming out from hiding.

A lost soul wailing your discordant tunes,
Concocted from the threads of your delusions,
Can you not see past the black clouds that contain you?

There is a world out there filled with new beginnings,
And people who could be your friends-
Though you keep running towards the skies.

A home exists where you could come alive-
So much to see, to hear and to touch…
You laugh cacophonously amidst
the ghosts of your phantasmal kingdom.
Open your eyes to envision true and harmonious daylight.

You chant, though without conviction to eerie tunes
That emanate from scratched records abrasively screeching on the phonograph.
One day you shall awaken inside of a bleak, tiled room
Sitting cross legged upon a cold metal floor behind locked doors.

Amidst whining dirges repeating in the darkness,
Not knowing if the sun is rising
Or if the moon has come out from hiding,
You shall be incongruously dancing
Beneath rapidly dimming fluorescent lights –alone.

Claudia A Krizay